KINGFISHER

First published 2011 by Kingfisher
an imprint of Macmillan Children's Books
a division of Macmillan Publishers Limited
20 New Wharf Road, London N1 9RR
Basingstoke and Oxford
Associated companies throughout the world
www.panmacmillan.com

ISBN 978-0-7534-3085-9

Consultant: Dr Troy P Regis

Designed and created by Basher www.basherbooks.com
Text written by Dan Green

Dedicated to Bill Penn and the Elephant Boys

Text and design copyright © Toucan Books Ltd. 2011
Based on an original concept by Toucan Books Ltd.
Illustrations copyright © Simon Basher 2011

9 8 7 6 5 4 3 2 1
1TR/0411/WKT/UNTD/140MA

A CIP catalogue record for this book
is available from the British Library.

Printed in China

Note to readers: the website addresses listed above are correct at
the time of going to print. However, due to the ever-changing nature
of the internet, website addresses and content can change. Websites
can contain links that are unsuitable for children. The publisher cannot
be held responsible for changes in website addresses or content, or for
information obtained through a third party. We strongly advise that
internet searches should be supervised by an adult.

CONTENTS

Introduction
Algebra and Geometry

Maths is all around you. There are treasures to count up and cakes to divide. You'll find number sequences in a sunflower's delicate spirals, in the honeycombs of busy bees and – watch out! – in the rapid spread of deadly bacteria. But hey, no matter what happens in *this* crazy, chaotic world, in peaceful Mathsland, two plus one is *always* three. Oh yeah, there's safety in numbers.

Pythagoras was an ancient Greek who loved to give his brain a good workout. Geometry kept his mind trim! He found out amazing stuff about numbers and shapes – most famously, his theorem on triangles. Algebra, with its *a*s, *b*s and *x*s, is simply a method of doing maths when you don't have all the facts to hand – kind of like detective work. Pythagoras understood that, although maths is counting and business and real-world things, it also exists in a world of its own. This means you can share ideas with anyone, no matter what language they speak. Even aliens! If extraterrestrials are smart enough to build a spaceship, chances are they'll also know how to count! Get ready to take things to the next level.

Pythagoras

Chapter 1
Counting Crew

Meet the gang who got this adventure going. And let's start with the amazing idea that a written symbol can stand in for something you can count. That's right! The Counting Crew began as scratches in stones or collections of sticks that somehow represented numbers. They've been around for "sum" time and they're clever fellas, too. You read numbers from left to right, like words, but you can tell the value of a number by working your way from right to left. The place value increases with each digit, to give you ones, tens, hundreds and so on. Make no mistake – these dudes are the maths symbols that count!

Roman Numerals

■ Counting Crew

✷ Numerals are symbols that are used to represent numbers
✷ This number system is fiendishly difficult to handle
✷ There is no Roman numeral for zero

I'm an ancient numbering system, dating back to the days when men wore skirts and sandals. I use capital letters for numbers: I=1; V=5; X=10; L=50; C=100; D=500; M=1000. Reading from the left, III=3, VII=7 and XX=20. But 4 is not IIII, it's IV! That's because a smaller value numeral *in front* of a large one tells you to subtract! So, IX=9 and XL=40. It makes me a devil to do sums with!

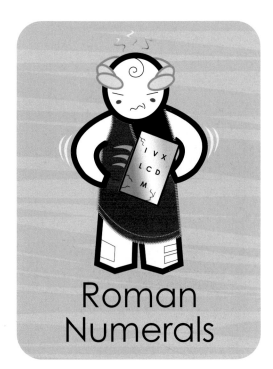

Roman Numerals

● Earliest known use: about 9BCE
● 1 to 10 in Roman numerals: I, II, III, IV, V, VI, VII, VIII, IX, X
● The "A" team: first XI (football); first XV (rugby union)

Arabic Numerals
Counting Crew

- ✹ Official international number system and language of maths
- ✹ Properly called Hindu-Arabic numerals
- ✹ First system to acknowledge zero as a number

Arabic Numerals

With roots in ancient Indian and Arabian trade and mathematics, I'm used the world over for measuring and counting. You know me – I'm the system of ten numbers you learn at school: 0, 1, 2, 3, 4, 5, 6, 7, 8 and 9. Each number has its own value, plus another value given by its position. Take 794: this means seven hundreds (7x100), nine tens (9x10) and four ones (4x1). Sure beats DCCXCIV*!

- ● Earliest known use: 500CE
- ● Multiples of 9 (18, 45, 198) also have digits that add up to a multiple of 9
- ● *DCCXCIV: the equivalent of 794 in Roman numerals

Zero

■ Counting Crew

☀ The number with the hole in the middle, aka nil or nought
☀ This out-for-a-duck digit helps make huge or tiny numbers
☀ The first even digit of the set of whole numbers

Think I'm nothin'? Think I ain't somethin'? Mr Unity puts it about like he's the Big Cheese, like he's the only one with any value. Well, I may be *worth* nothin', but I *mean* a lot. Just let me loose with my mates, Arabic Numerals and Base 10, and you'll see all sorts of maths mastery.

After 9 comes 10: it's me that signals a change of place value from ones to tens (in this case) or tens to hundreds and so on. When I follow a number I make it ten times bigger – 2 becomes 20, then 200, then 2000. Add me to a number and nothing happens, but subtract a number from *me* and you'll dive into Negative Number's murky depths. Multiply a number by me and I make it disappear. Ask me to divide, though, and I'll create mathematical mayhem. Man, I've got zero tolerance for that!

● First recorded use: 458CE
● $x^0=1$ (in other words, any number to the power of zero = 1)
● Googol: 1 followed by one hundred zeros

Zero

Unity
■ Counting Crew

- ✳ This special one is the number between 0 and 2
- ✳ The first positive odd number
- ✳ In probability, 1 is a 100% likely chance – a certainty

I am your Number One, the top of the pile, the king of the maths mountain. Tall and slender, I'm what every number longs to be. I'm the first non-zero whole number.

My maths wizardry is simply beguiling. Just think of the biggest number you can, then add 1. See? Adding me to any number makes it bigger and bigger and bigger, ever closer to infinity. I'm not a composite number, nor am I a prime number. I can change Odd Number into Even Number and Even into Odd. Integers (whole numbers) are always divisible by me. And I'm unique in that any number multiplied by me is itself – even me: I am my own square, my own cube, my own fourth power and so on (1x1=1; 1x1x1=1). I'm the only *one* who can say this and my Unity comes from being so pure. It's mystifying!

- ● Factor: a number by which a larger number can be divided equally
- ● Prime number: has only two factors (1 and itself, e.g. 13)
- ● Composite number: has more than two factors, e.g. 12 (1, 2, 3, 4, 6, 12)

Unity

13

Negative Number
Counting Crew

- ☀ Natural numbers are those above zero, used for counting
- ☀ This *unnatural* critter is lower in value than zero
- ☀ Always starts with a minus sign

They say I'm not natural and that I bring the number world down. It's just not fair. They make me wear a minus sign (–) and that's a real downer, too. OK, OK, I know I've got negative vibes, but you'd have them if you had to live in this chilly sub-zero zone. It's *brrr*, no doubt!

I'm what happens if you try to subtract a big number from a smaller one. It's something you can't do in the real world (just try to take nine sweets from a bag that has only five in it). In mind-bending Mathsland, however, nothing could be easier. You think Arabic Numerals stop at Zero? No sir, they get to Zero and just keep going – *backwards*: 0, –1, –2, –3. Take nine from six and you get minus three; add three to minus three and you get zero. You're right, there's nothing natural in that!

- ● A negative number x a positive number = a negative number
- ● A negative number ÷ a positive number = a negative number
- ● A negative number x/÷ a negative number = a positive number

Negative Number

Base 2

Counting Crew

- ✳ "Base" simply means how far you count before repeating
- ✳ Computers do their calculations using base 2
- ✳ Also known as the binary system

I work with two numbers – 0 and 1 – and each place value *doubles* as you work to the left. So, the last number on the right counts ones, the next to the left counts twos, then fours, then eights and so on. With me? C'mon, it's easy: 10 in base 2 (10_2) equals 2. That's because the 0 means no ones and the 1 means one two. It's pretty "base"-ic really. You try, with 10011_2*.

Base 2

- ● First known use: around 100BCE (India)
- ● Numbers 1 to 10 in base 2: 1, 10, 11, 100, 101, 110, 111, 1000, 1001, 1010
- ● *$10011_2 = (1\times16)+(0\times8)+(0\times4)+(1\times2)+(1\times1)=19$

Base 10

Counting Crew

* System that counts in sets of ten, tallying ones, tens, hundreds
* A natural way of counting that uses the tips of your ten digits
* Also known as the decimal system

Base 10

When it comes to getting somewhere with numbers, you can sure *count* on me to help. I work in sets of ten, where each place is ten times the value of the one to its right. It might sound tricky, but really it isn't. See, 39 means three tens and nine ones. The position containing the 3 (tens) is worth ten times the position containing the 9 (ones). Now that's gotta be worth some at-"ten"-tion!

* First known use: around 540BCE (China)
* Also referred to as powers of 10: $1093 = (1 \times 10^3) + (0 \times 10^2) + (9 \times 10^1) + (3 \times 10^0)$
* Digit comes from the Latin word for finger (*digitus*)

Significant Figure
■ Counting Crew

✴ This confident dude helps tidy up unnecessary extra digits
✴ Shortened to sig. fig. or s.f. for ease of use
✴ Not to be confused with decimal place

I'm your straight-dealing, no-nonsense kinda operator, sifting out unhelpful information to give you useful, relevant numbers. I help exercise a little control!

If I told you 5200 people attended a gig, would you think that exactly 5200 came? No! You'd know this was an estimate given to the nearest hundred. This calculation is up to me, and written using sig. figs.* The *precise* number of people may not be known or relevant, so I round up or down to tell you *roughly* how many people came, while still being accurate enough to use! (The actual number is between 5100 and 5300 since I have two sig. figs.) My rules are simple: the first non-zero digit in a number is the first sig. fig.; the second is the next and so on. This means that 0.005108 has the same number of sig. figs. as 3007 (four).

● To find a sig. fig., use the next digit for rounding up or down: 4.067=4.07 (3 s.f.)
● Round up with a next digit of 5 or over, otherwise round down: 4.064=4.06 (3 s.f.)
● *5183 people attended the gig, so 5200 has been rounded up to two sig. figs.

Significant Figure

Chapter 2
Number Nutters

Meet the Number Nutters, a *prime* bunch indeed! Here you've got solid, dependable Integer, Even Steven and reasonable Rational Number. Look closer, and you'll also find quirky and radical Odd, Irrational and Imaginary Numbers among their ranks. And lurking between them all are those bit-players, Fraction and Decimal. Underestimate this crew at your peril! It's bursting at the seams – count up from Zero and you'll see there are gazillions of them. You can't even list all the numbers from 0 to 1 – there's 0.1, but also 0.11 and 0.111 and 0.1111 and… feeling number nutty? Don't let these guys do a number on you!

Integer

Even Number

Odd Number

Prime Number

Power

Fraction

Decimal

Rational
Number

Irrational
Number

Imaginary
Number

Integer

Number Nutters

* All whole numbers, including zero, are integers
* Can be positive or negative (excluding zero)
* You round a decimal number up (or down) to make it whole

Well-rounded and complete, I have got it sussed. The full-fat digit with no messy fractions or trailing decimal parts, I am your bona fide whole number.

I've got my feet firmly on the ground, helping you to count real-life things – stuff like ice-cream cones, friends and skateboards. Say, when did you last hear of half a telephone or 4.3 trucks? Exactly! You simply can't get enough of my wholesome goodness. My pals and I go into infinity and some of us even claim to be perfect! Oh yeah, a perfect number is very special indeed. Its proper factors add up to its sum. Take the number 6, for example: its proper factors are 1, 2 and 3. Add these up and you get 6. Completely useless, but utterly satisfying! See if you can find the next one*.

● Proper factors: the numbers by which a figure can be divided, excluding itself
● **Z**: the set of all integers where, for example, Z_{10} is the set of integers from 1 to 9
● *Next perfect number: 28 (1+2+4+7+14)

Integer

Even Number

Number Nutters

✳ Any integer that ends in 0, 2, 4, 6 or 8
✳ Can always be divided into two equal parts
✳ All known perfect numbers are even and end in 6 or 8

Hey there. I'm Mr Trustworthy, the honest guy, the good cop. You can always count on me to play it by the book. Unlike elusive Prime Number and quirky Odd, I am easy to work with. Even Steven, that's me.

I like to keep things nice and tidy. Chop me into two exact same halves and I guarantee you'll never find any remainders – not a single one! Oh no, I always finish up my plate, no leftovers here. Makes perfect sense, doesn't it? Because I'm easy to split into equal parts, you'll never have any trouble finding some of my factors. Those are the numbers that will divide me exactly. (One of them will always be 2, for starters.) You see, I'm not very tricky and I don't try to catch you out or rock the boat. Life is so much easier when you stay on an *even* keel!

● Adding two even numbers together = an even number
● Adding two odd numbers together = an even number
● Any two even numbers multiplied together = an even number

Even Number

Odd Number

Number Nutters

* Any integer that ends in 1, 3, 5, 7 and 9
* Can't be divided into two equal parts without a remainder
* No known perfect numbers are odd

I'm a funny fish, me, the odd bod who simply refuses to be divided by two without there being something left over. Take number 7, for example: 7 divided by 2 equals 3... plus 1; OK, er, 23 divided by 2 equals 11... mmm, plus 1 again. That's odd, you might say, there's always a one left over, a remainder. But that's just how I operate: that's me.

And where would you be without me? You see, Even Number counts up in steps of two, but what happens in between? Well, that's where things start to get interesting. It's me that fills the gaps to give you three's company, the fifth element, seventh heaven and unlucky (for some) thirteen. Want to know what makes me a real oddity, though? Try taking one odd number from another – say 5 from 11. I know! It's even! Now that really *is* odd.

● Adding two odd numbers together = an even number
● Subtracting one odd number from another = an even number
● Any two odd numbers multiplied together = an odd number

Odd Number

Prime Number
Number Nutters

* A number that can be divided evenly *only* by 1 and itself
* A positive integer that is not a prime is a composite number
* 1 is not a prime number because it only has one divisor (1)

I am one choice cut! Built like an American footballer, I'm the beefcake of the Number Nutters and a nice meaty subject to get your teeth into, believe me.

To join my club, a number must have just two divisors. Try to find factors for one of my gang, say 13: 6x2=12 (too low) and 7x2=14 (too high). The only combination of numbers multiplied together that will give you 13 is 1x13. So, now you know I'm exclusive, but did you know that I'm also elusive? Oh yeah, finding new primes is a favourite brain-busting activity for maths geeks. There are an infinite number, but no one has developed a foolproof method for finding them. The largest known Prime to date contains almost 13 million digits, enough to fill more than 500 Basher books! I'm in my *prime*, I tell you!

● First eleven prime numbers: 2, 3, 5, 7, 11, 13, 17, 19, 23, 29, 31
● Only even prime number: 2
● Magic prime: 73939133 (makes a new prime with each digit taken from the end)

Prime Number

Power
Number Nutters

- ☀ A handy method of repeat multiplication
- ☀ Also known as exponentiation
- ☀ Deals in whopping numbers but also extremely titchy ones

I'm mathematical dynamite! I'm marked out by my exponent, which is written above, and to the right, of a number. I'm only small, but boy do I pack a punch – fire me up and I'll be belting out big numbers in no time.

My job is to multiply a number by itself again and again. Take diddy number 5, for example: 5^2 (five to the power of two or five squared) means 5x5, which is 25; but $5^3 =$ 5x5x5=125; and 5^4=5x5x5x5=625. See how quickly I reach eye-wateringly vast extremes! And I work both ways – if my exponent is a negative number, I get exceedingly tiny (although I never drop below zero). For example 10^{-5} is 0.00001. You'll find me all over the place, especially in science, where I offer a neat way to write down huge and tiny numbers. Powerful stuff!

- ● Any number raised to the power of 1 is the number itself: 3^1 is the same as 1x3
- ● Smallest 5th power, other than 1: 32 (2^5 or 2x2x2x2x2)
- ● Googolplex: 10^{googol} or 1 followed by 10^{100} zeros

Power

Fraction
Number Nutters

✳ This broken figure is more than zero, but less than one
✳ Written as a numerator over a denominator: $^1/_2$, for example
✳ Used to express a proportion of something or a percentage

Some say I should be sad because I'm broken, because I'm just a *fraction* of the number I used to be. Well, I may be divided, but I can still conquer. Let me tell you why.

Written like this: $^2/_3$, my numerator tells you how many equal portions I contain (two), while my denominator tells you how many equal parts make up a whole (three). It's a neat little system that leaves Decimal floundering! You see, $^2/_3$ also means 2÷3, but pop that into a calculator and you get 0.6666666 – ugh, that's messy! And check this out: you can compare two fractions by finding the lowest common denominator. Take $^5/_6$ and $^7/_9$. Both denominators go equally into 18 (6x3; 9x2). Multiplying the top number by the same figure in each case (5x3; 7x2) makes $^{15}/_{18}$ and $^{14}/_{18}$, so $^5/_6$ is "fraction"-ally the bigger portion.

● Proper fraction: numerator smaller than denominator ($^3/_5$)
● Improper fraction: numerator larger than denominator ($^7/_5$)
● Mixed number: whole number plus proper fraction ($1^2/_5$)

Fraction

Decimal
Number Nutters

* Form of not-whole number that is expressed using a full stop
* Takes its name from the Latin for tenth: *decimus*
* Works hand-in-hand with base 10

Hi, I'm Decimal, your pocket calculator pal. Just punch in 0.7734 and turn that gizmo upside down to get a big hello from me! Welcome to my universe.

Like Fraction, I inhabit the vast worlds that exist between whole numbers, but I'm more methodical than that slap-dash dandy. Instead of denominators of all sizes, I use powers of ten. This means I can convert stack-'em-high fractions into lovely decimal-digit strings. I transform $^4/_5$ into a neat 0.8, which ('cos you're pretty darn clever) you'll see is the same as $^8/_{10}$ or 8÷10. With me, messy mixed numbers, such as $3^1/_{12}$, are a thing of the past (3.083), and percentages a cinch. Just look at 0.75 and you can see straight away that it is $^{75}/_{100}$, or 75%. Try 0.04*. That's me – a straight-talking guy who likes to get to the point!

● Earliest known use: 1BCE (China)
● $^1/_2$=0.5
● *0.04 as a percentage: 4%

Decimal

Rational Number

Number Nutters

☀ Any number that can also be written as a fraction
☀ Finishes neatly, or ends with a repeating pattern of numbers
☀ Includes all base 10 and base 2 numbers

I'm a reasonable chap – I just like to see a pattern emerging. Rational, in maths, refers to the ratio of two whole numbers – one divided by the other. My great pals are Integer, who is always divisible by 1 ($^{13}/_1$ is just 13, isn't it?), and Fraction – simply one integer over another. OK, so $^2/_9$ makes a long repeating pattern in Decimal's hands*, but it is a pattern none the less.

Rational
Number

● $^{62}/_{99}$=0.62626262626
● **Q**: the symbol used to denote the set of all rational numbers
● *2÷9=0.222222222222222222

Irrational Number

Number Nutters

* Any number that cannot be written as a fraction
* Has an infinitely long decimal tail that never repeats
* Significantly more numbers are irrational than rational

Irrational
Number

I'm a silly sprout that simply *can't* be written down as one whole number divided by another. Divide 4 by 1 and you get 0.25 – a nice, well-rounded, rational decimal. But there's no end to my trailing decimal digits, and no repeating patterns either – count backwards and you'll still be going at the end of time. My best buddies are Square Root, Pi and e. You should check 'em out.

- $\sqrt{2}$: 1.414213562373095...
- Pi (π): 3.141592653589793...
- e: 2.718281828459045...

Imaginary Number
Number Nutters

✴ One of maths' most baffling concepts
✴ Used with real numbers to form complex numbers
✴ Labelled *i* to mean the square root of −1 ($\sqrt{-1}$)

Man the mizzenmasts and set sail for strange lands of mathematical mystery! I'm a buccaneer of the bizarre – a totally unreal adventurer. My numbers don't belong to the real world of biscuits and buttons, but they are concrete and countable nevertheless... stick with it!

You can tell if a number is imaginary, because it has an *i* after it (2*i*), where the *i* is defined as $\sqrt{-1}$. And $\sqrt{-1}$ must be imaginary, mustn't it, because the square of any number is always positive, isn't it? Well, test it out: −1x−1=+1. Mmm, yet my feet are firmly in the real world. Complex numbers, with their real and imaginary dimensions (5+2*i*), are perfect for describing electromagnetic radiation, such as sunlight or radio waves. I explode so many knotty real-world problems, I'm a weapon of *math* destruction!

● $i^2 = -1$ (*i* x *i*, or *i* squared = −1)
● Inventor of *i* symbol: Leonhard Euler (1777)
● Euler's Theory: $e^{\pi i} = -1$ (e to the power of pi and *i* = −1)

Imaginary Number

Chapter 3
Cranium Crackers

This gang of braincase busters is awesome. The Cranium Crackers challenge you to use the stuffing between your lugholes – no room for puddin' heads here! A cracking mix of extraordinary equations, fabulous functions and punchy processes, these guys have amazing power to change numbers, shunt them about, split them up and juggle them around. You will use each of them again and again when you do algebra, so find out how and why each of them operates (and how to reverse it). Before you know it, you'll be chipping away at tricky conundrums as if they were cheap crockery!

Factor

Product

Square

Cube

Square Root

Cube Root

Equation

Simultaneous Equation

Factor

■ Cranium Crackers

✳ A positive integer that divides a larger number evenly
✳ Has no messy leftovers or remainders
✳ A number with factors of just 1 and itself is a prime number

Aka The Divisor, I'm a mean, green calculatin' machine. I blast a number into smaller, equal-sized portions. Because there are often more than two ways to divide a number like this, the bigger the number, the more of me there are. For example, the number 9 has three factors (1, 3 and 9), while 32 has six factors (1, 2, 4, 8, 16 and 32).

Working out factors of really big numbers is as easy as nailing jelly to the wall. It takes some serious number crunching. The best way to do it is to split a number into its prime factors. Taking 737 and starting with the smallest prime numbers, you find that 737 will not divide by 2, 3, 5 or 7, but 11x67=737. It doesn't divide evenly by any other prime. So, 737 is a composite number with just four factors – 1, 11, 67 and 737. Consider it crunched!

● If a number ends in 5 or 0, one of its factors is certainly 5
● Composite: the name given to a number with more than two factors
● Prime factor: any factor that is also a prime number

Factor

Product
Cranium Crackers

☀ The mathematical opposite of factor
☀ Also referred to as the result of one number times another
☀ Almost always a composite number, and sometimes a prime

Hi, I'm Product, chalk to Factor's mathematical cheese, and Tom to his arithmetical Jerry. Whereas Factor is all about dividing numbers down to their smallest parts, I'm what you get when you multiply numbers together. Take 5x6 and you get a *product* of 30.

My job is all about thinking BIG (unless Negative Number happens to be involved)! And I'm hardly giving away any secrets when I say that numbers multiplied together to make a product are also the factors of that same product. I produce composite numbers – that is, any positive whole numbers with more factors than 1 and the number itself. Making prime numbers is more tricky, because the only way to do it is by using 1 as a factor. Take 13. I can only make 13 as a product by multiplying 13 by 1 (13x1=13).

● Factorial (n!): product of the integers equal to and less than *n*
● 2 factorial (2!): 2 (2x1)
● 5 factorial (5!): 120 (5x4x3x2x1)

Product

Square

■ Cranium Crackers

☀ A number multiplied by itself
☀ A special case of power, where the index is two
☀ The mathematical opposite of square root

Call me Square Pants if you like, but I'm far from boring. The littlest of the Power pals, I'm a number raised to the power of two (that is, multiplied by itself). Two squared is 2^2. It's the same as 2x2=4. I'm always positive* – but you know that by now. When I square Odd Number the result is odd, while squares of Even Number are even. I have my uses, so you'd better *square* up.

Square

● Units squared are used to measure area – for example, cm^2
● All squares end in a repeating pattern: 00, 1, 4, 9, 6, 25, 6, 9, 4, 1, 00
● *3^2(3x3)=9 and -3^2(−3x−3)=9

Cube
Cranium Crackers

- A number multiplied by itself and then again
- A special case of power, where the power index is three
- The mathematical opposite of cube root

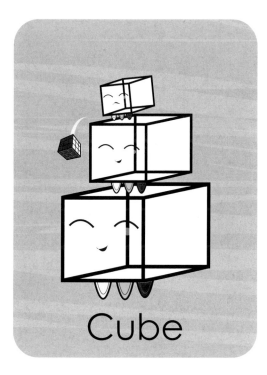

Cube

Imagine a Rubik's Cube and you've got me – a solid shape where each side is equal to three units. Officially, I'm a number raised to the power of three. This just means a number multiplied by itself and then multiplied by itself again. Two cubed is 2^3, which is the same as 2x2x2=8. There's more to me than my bro, Square, and, unlike him, I can be a little negative* at times.

- Units multiplied in three dimensions give you the volume of a solid shape
- Smallest cube that is a sum of two different cubes is 1729: $1^3+12^3=9^3+10^3$
- *3^3(3x3x3)=27 but -3^3(−3x−3x−3)=−27

Square Root
■ Cranium Crackers

✳ This cheeky scamp is the mathematical opposite of square
✳ The square root of −1 ($\sqrt{-1}$) is an imaginary number (*i*)
✳ A natural number has a positive and a negative square root

A mathematical monkey, I swing my cheeky tail over a number to undo Square's multiplication: $4^2=16$ and $\sqrt{16}=4$. The definition for $\sqrt{x}$ is the number whose square equals x: so $\sqrt{16}=4$. When given a perfect square like 16, I'll make a lovely rational number (4). But try me on non-perfect squares – say, 15* – and I'll give you endless (literally) irrational numbers.

Square Root

● Earliest known use: between 1800 BCE and 1600 BCE (Babylon)
● $\sqrt{x}=x^{1/2}$
● *$\sqrt{15}$=3.872983346207416...

Cube Root
Cranium Crackers

✴ This egghead is the mathematical opposite of cube
✴ Cube roots of non-perfect cubes are irrational numbers
✴ Any (real) number has only one cube root

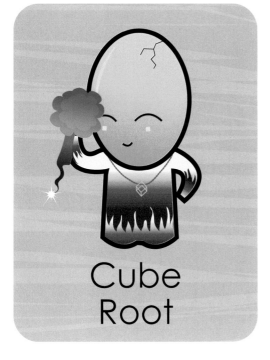

Cube
Root

Like Square Root, I'm a real hotshot, busy undoing all of Cube's hard work. See how quick I unpick Cube's multiplication: $4^3=64$ and $\sqrt[3]{64}=4$. Ha ha. Nothing could be easier, could it? The definition for $\sqrt[3]{x}$ is the number whose cube equals x: so $\sqrt[3]{64}=4$. Unlike Square, I can only ever have one root – I'll have none of this positive/negative roots business, no sir!

● First demonstrated by Galileo (1638)
● $\sqrt[3]{x}=x^{1/3}$
● On a calculator: press √, x, √√, x, √√√, x, etc, until the number doesn't change

Equation
Cranium Crackers

* Algebraic method where letters replace unknown numbers
* Defines a relationship between one or more variables
* Expressions on either side of equal signs have the same value

I've got a bad rep for being a complicated brain-acher. But given the chance, I can show you how to use letters instead of numbers to think in a new and exciting way.

Sometimes, you have an answer but don't know the question. At such times, my letters stand in for the numbers that you don't know. Say Tyson is 4 years old and Rosie is 26. At what age will Rosie be three times Tyson's age? Well, in x years from now, Tyson will be 4+x and Rosie will be 26+x. Written as an equation, she will be three times older than him when $3(4+x)=26+x$. You can eliminate the numbers that you *do* know by writing the same equation like this: $26-(3\times4)=2x$. So now you know that $14=2x$, which means that $x=7$. When Tyson is 11, Rosie will be 33. It's as easy as a, b, c – or should I say x, y, z!

● A linear equation has only one value of x that will solve it
● A quadratic equation is one that involves a square
● A cubic equation is one that involves a cube

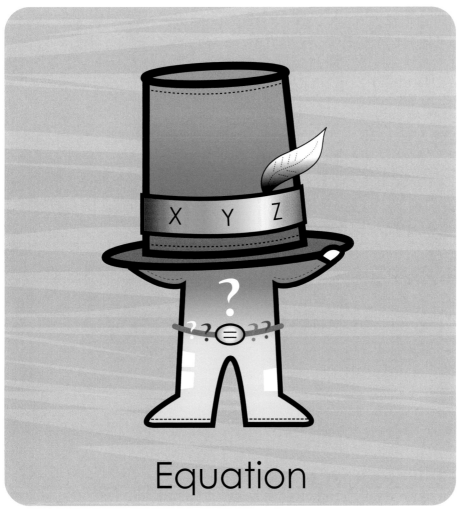

Equation

Simultaneous Equation

Cranium Crackers

✳ Finds solutions for two (or more) separate equations
✳ Works by substituting one equation into another
✳ Can also be solved by plotting it on a graph

I am algebra's elder statesman, a multi-tasker whose left hand *always* knows what the right hand is doing. I help out when two (or more) equations need a mutual solution.

When faced with two equations, say $3x+2y=8$ and $x+4y=6$, you must first know that solutions exist that make them *both* true. The key is to isolate one of the variables. In this case $3x+2y=8$ looks tricky, but $x+4y=6$ can be rewritten as $x=6-4y$ (isolating the x). The first equation can now read as $3(6-4y)+2y=8$. Distributing the 3 on the brackets gives you $18-12y+2y=8$. Simplified further, this is $18-10y=8$, which can also be written $10y=18-8$. This means that $10y=10$, so $y=1$. Now *you* return to the second equation to find x*!

● First known use: c.1950BCE (Babylon)
● Father of algebra: Muhammad ibn Musa al-Khwarizmi (c.780–850CE)
● *$x+4y=6$: $x+(4\times1)=6$, so $x+4=6$ or $x=6-4$; $x=2$

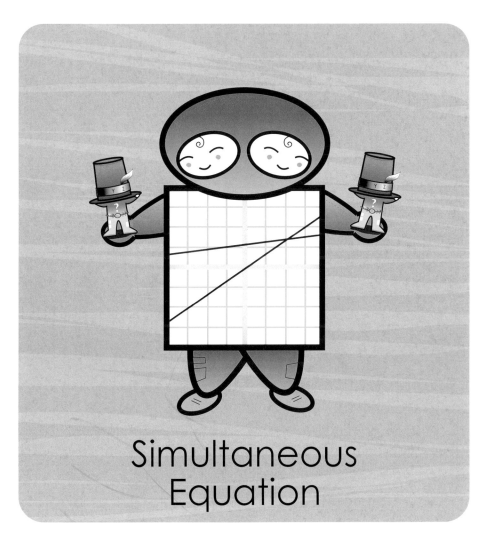

Simultaneous
Equation

Chapter 4
Graph Gang

Bring out the Graph Gang! This hands-on bunch of mathematical wonders simply love to roll up their sleeves, sharpen their pencils and get something down on graph paper. These guys prove the point that by far the best way to visualize a maths formula is to do so graphically. It's a team effort with stalwarts Line, Plane and Function *coordinating* (geddit?) their energies to show the relationship between two (or more) variables in an equation (that is, how *y* varies with *x*). Literally *drawing* together their incredible powers makes them ace for analyzing data. Seeing really *is* believing!

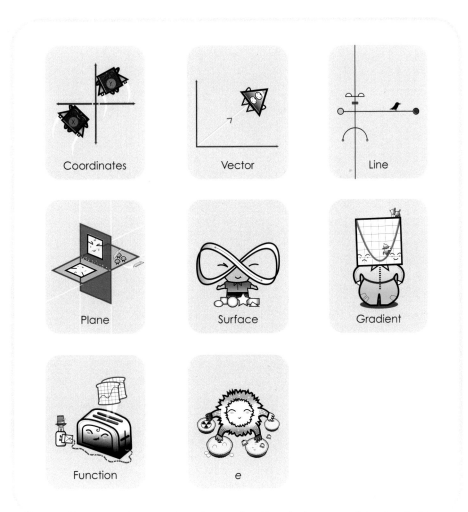

Coordinates

Vector

Line

Plane

Surface

Gradient

Function

e

Coordinates
Graph Gang

* Pairs of numbers, written (x,y), locating position
* The x-axis is horizontal and the y-axis is vertical
* They provide grid references so that mapmaking is possible

Location, location, location – it's what we're all about. You see, we provide a system for pinpointing a position. It's great, you'll never be lost with us around!

We're called x and y, and although we're diddy, the Graph Gang would get nowhere without us. Every single one of them needs *us* to be able to conduct their operations. This is how we work: x is positioned on the horizontal axis, while y is positioned on the vertical axis. The point at which our lines cross gives a position, which is written down as two numbers inside round brackets, separated by a comma: (4,3) or (−5,7). Our values are written in alphabetical order, so the first number refers to the x coordinate and the second number to the y coordinate. Oh yeah, we've got it all mapped out!

● Inventor: René Descartes (17th century)
● Formal name: Cartesian coordinates (from Descartes)
● The coordinates (0,0) are labelled "the origin"

Coordinates

Vector
Graph Gang

- ✹ A line on a graph that has magnitude (size) and direction
- ✹ Works with coordinates to get from point to point on a graph
- ✹ Vectors with the same magnitude and direction are equal

I'm a zippy little fella that's drawn as a straight line on a graph. I get you from point to point using the shortest distance and, believe me, I know where I'm going!

I'm a double-decker, written with one number plonked above the other in brackets. I use my pals, Coordinates, with my x value above my y value. So $\left(\begin{smallmatrix}3\\4\end{smallmatrix}\right)$ means move three across to the right (in a positive x direction) and move four up the y-axis. When you see me on a graph, there's a chevron, or arrow, drawn on my line to indicate direction. The very same line in the opposite direction is $\left(\begin{smallmatrix}-3\\-4\end{smallmatrix}\right)$, and has a downward-pointing arrow. I can be added, subtracted *and* multiplied – engineers adore me! They use me to calculate the results of forces acting in different directions. Don't hector this Vector!

- ● Vector graphics: computer images drawn using geometry rather than pixels
- ● First video game: Spacewar! (Steve "Slug" Russell, 1961)
- ● First vector graphics drawing program: Sketchpad (1963)

Vector

Line
Graph Gang

- ☀ A one-dimensional character of infinite length
- ☀ Linear functions (equations) draw clean, straight lines
- ☀ Quadratic and cubic functions draw lovely curves

I'm a slip of a lad, me – the skinniest beanpole you ever did see. I'm so thin, I exist in one dimension only! I have no width or depth, only length. But no matter how flimsy and wobbly you think I am, there's not a shape or function that can be drawn without me.

I can be straight or bendy. When I'm straight, I take the shortest route between two points (like Vector), while my curved versions arc elegantly across the page. I am drawn towards other lines (unless they are parallel, two straight lines always meet). And when I intersect, or cross, another line, I make an angle – for example, perpendicular lines meet at right angles (90°). Meanwhile, parallel lines run like train tracks – on and on, side by side, never getting closer to each other and never getting further away. Ahh!

- ● Line segment: a line of fixed length with two end points
- ● Hyperbola and parabola: names given to special curved lines
- ● Spirangle: a spiral made using straight lines

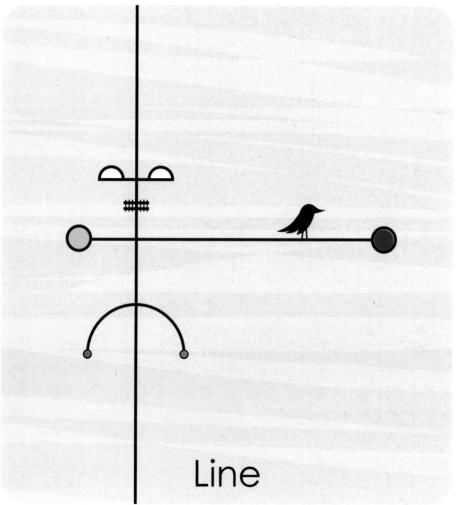

Line

Plane
Graph Gang

- ☀ A 2D surface of infinite area and zero thickness
- ☀ Two non-parallel planes will always intersect along a line
- ☀ A line can intersect a plane, run parallel to it or be part of it

Imagine a wall, floor or ceiling stretching out forever in every direction to make me: beautiful Plane. Mmm, no doubt you are looking at that wall, floor or ceiling, all flat and featureless, and wondering what's so special. But, really, there's more to me than meets the eye.

You see, a graph – most geometry in fact – is carried out in the plane: lines are drawn across my surface. Like Line, I can be parallel, where one plane sits above another, like stacked sheets of paper. They never get closer to each other, or move farther away and most certainly do not touch! I also intersect with other planes to make solid shapes with flat surfaces. Perpendicular planes intersect at right angles to make cuboid shapes, but I can also make prisms and pyramids. You see, I'm no *plane* Jane after all!

- ● World's largest ice rink: 165,600 m² (Rideau Canal Skateway, Canada)
- ● World's largest flat-screen TV: 4.8x2.4 m (Technovision Luxio)
- ● World's longest covered outdoor escalator system: 800 m (Hong Kong)

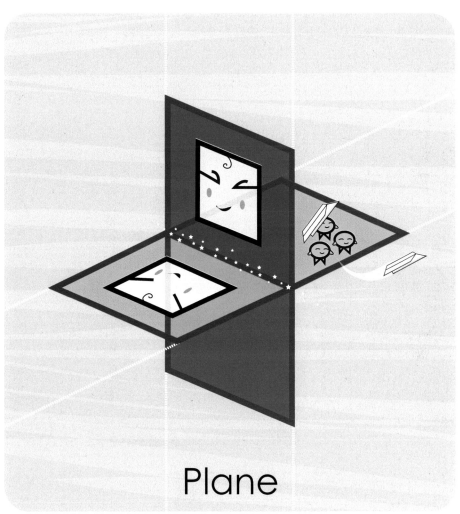

Plane

Surface
Graph Gang

☀ A 2D area of zero thickness, sometimes curved in 3D space
☀ Stretches like a skin over every 3D shape
☀ Surfaces with edges and a fixed area are said to be "closed"

Check me out! I'm the ultimate in geometry flamboyancy. Maths geeks go gaga for my curves! Unlike simpletons Line and Plane, I can also work in three dimensions.

I make up the outer walls of a solid shape: every single object has me stretched over its outsides. While you can visualize Plane with something as disappointing as a wall, you can picture my sweeping curves on a rounded shape like a cylinder. Wanna see a trick? Take a long strip of paper, twist it in the middle and join the ends together to make a loop. Run your finger all the way around that loop and you'll see that you've made a special shape with only one surface. While fun, this frivolity merely scratches at the *surface* of the computing and engineering applications I can help with.

● First described: c.300BCE (Euclid)
● Surface area of a cube: $6s^2$ (s is length of one side)
● Total surface area of an average adult brain: 2500 cm^2

Surface

Gradient
Graph Gang

- ✳ The slope of a line on a graph
- ✳ A positive gradient slopes up from left to right
- ✳ A negative gradient slides down from left to right

Hey, come climb with me, the concept with very real effects. The bigger the gradient of a hill, the steeper it is and the more you'll sweat as you go! There's no *sloping* about here – this ride is for mountain goats only!

I'm a cinch to calculate. The gradient of a slope – real or mathematical, steep or shallow – is the ratio between how far you climb up (the vertical, y component) and the distance you travel forward (the horizontal, x component). In maths language, this is written $(y_2-y_1)/(x_2-x_1)$. To find the gradient of a straight line, therefore, all you do is find two points on it and work out the difference between their y and x components. Say the two points were (3,2) and (8,4). I would be $^{4-2}/_{8-3}=^2/_5=0.4$ (also written as two in five, 2:5 or 40%). Well, get moving! Can you make the grade?

- ● Gradient of 1 is equal to a 45° angle on a standard coordinate grid
- ● Steepest (non-rack) train track: 0.135 (13.5%) Lisbon, Portugal
- ● Steepest rack railway: 0.48 (48%) Pilatus Mountain Railway, Switzerland

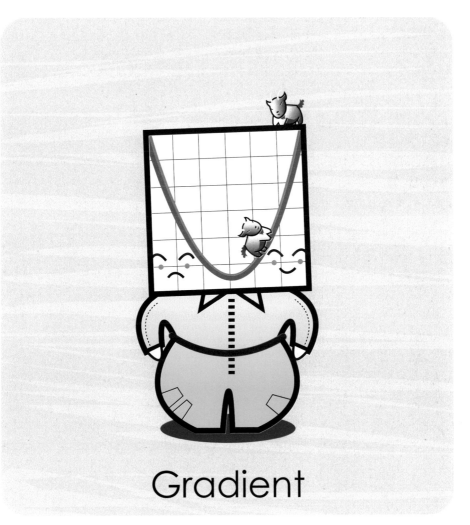

Gradient

Function
Graph Gang

☀ A formula that converts one value into another
☀ An inverse function reverses the operation
☀ All functions are equations, but not all equations are functions

I'm an operator, a hustler, a mathematical string-puller. I work the numbers, taking one value and changing it into another. I am written as $f(x)$, which is spoken as "eff of ex". Whenever you see me, you know you are looking at an equation of some kind, written in terms of x. Put simply, plug x into the equation, and out pops an answer.

There's nothing to be scared of here. My operations can be as simple as adding 1 to a number. Take $f(x)=3x+1$: if x is 7, $f(x)=22$ (that is, $3 \times 7+1$). Easy, right? Loads of guys in this book can be described as forms of me: Square, Cube, Sine, Cosine, Tangent, Square Root, Cube Root – they're all functions! Square is just an easier way of saying $f(x)=x$ times x. I come into my own on a graph, helping to draw all manner of lines, curves and shapes.

● First use of the word function: 1673 (Gottfried Leibniz)
● Linear functions (x) produce straight-line graphs
● Quadratic functions (x^2) produce parabolic graphs

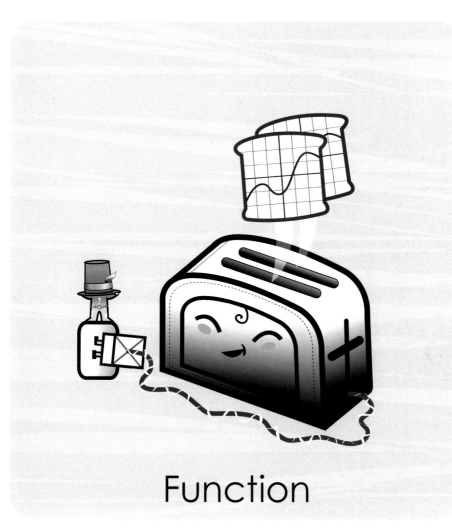

Function

e

Graph Gang

* The most important and useful constant in maths
* Defined as the limit of $(1+{}^1/_n)^n$ as n goes to infinity
* Crops up anywhere there is growth or decay

A relative newcomer to maths, I am sparky and vibrant. My proper name is Euler's Number (after that brainy fellow, Leonhard Euler, who investigated my many and various uses). You can call me e. I am the most important number, along with 0 (Zero), 1 (Unity), π (Pi) and i (Imaginary Number). Like my good friend Pi, I am a mathematical constant and an Irrational Number to boot!

I'm used for measuring things that grow continuously and I put a limit on how fast they flourish. And, believe me, I've got a finger in many pies. Give me half a chance and I'll tell you how radioactive decay slows down or the maximum your money can earn in a bank. I can even be used to find out how quickly a deadly virus could spread. All together now – "For e's a jolly good fellow!"

● Discoverer: Jacob Bernoulli (1727)
● Euler's Number (e): 2.71828182845904523536…
● Known digits of e: 1,000,000,000,000 decimal places (Kondo & Yee, 2010)

e

Chapter 5
Shape Sisters

What a bevy of beauties the Shape Sisters are, with the lovely Polygon leading by example. Lying flat on a 2D plane, Polygon is made with straight lines that meet at points, or vertices. The smallest shape that can be made in this way is a triangle (spot the family connection with the Trig-Athletes). Besides shapely shapes, this sisterhood embraces 1D Perimeter, 2D and 3D spaceheads Area and Volume, and playful, pattern-making Tessellation. Together they let you explore the world of shapes – for example, out of all four-sided shapes with the same Perimeter, a square has the largest Area. Square that!

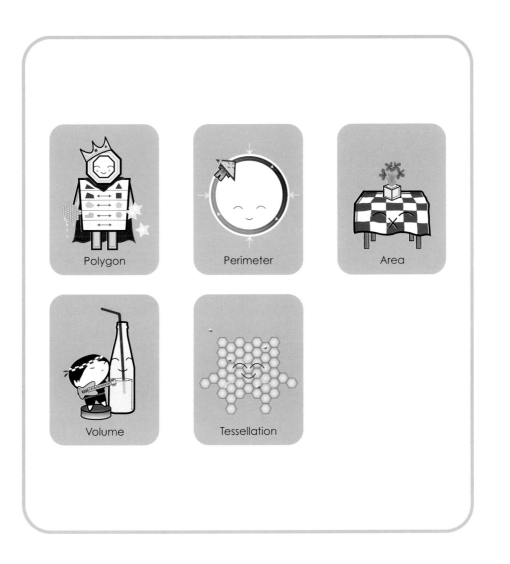

Polygon

Perimeter

Area

Volume

Tessellation

Polygon
▪ Shape Sisters

✷ A shape made using points, straight lines and angles
✷ Each point, or corner, on a polygon is called a vertex
✷ From the Greek *polygon*, meaning figure with many angles

All hail the queen of the 2D flatlands! I am known as the set of all shapes, which means that every shape you can think of that is made with straight lines is one of me. You could say I'm the *shape* of things to come. Ha ha!

I can be regular or irregular, and it doesn't take long to spot the difference. Irregular, and I'm a ragbag jumble with sides of different lengths and skewiff interior angles. Regular, though, and there's a little more finesse: sides are all exactly the same length and all interior angles are equal. You'll see regular polygons everywhere – in starfruit (pentagon) and honeycombs (hexagon), for example. When laid next to each other, some shapes of the same kind fit together snugly with no gaps. It's a great game that Tessellation will tell you all about later on.

● *n*-gon: a polygon with *n* sides (*pentagon*, 5; *hexagon*, 6)
● All interior angles of a quadrilateral must add up to 360°
● Polyhedron (*pl.* polyhedra): a solid whose faces are polygons

Polygon

Perimeter
Shape Sisters

* The distance around the outside of an area
* Without this boundary, there is no shape
* The perimeter of a circle is known as its circumference

Come on out, I've got you surrounded! No, seriously, just giving you the runaround. It's what I do – I draw a line that encloses a shape to form its outline. I give a shape definition. That's me, a real mover and a shaper!

I'm just the thing you need for working out the area of chicken wire for your rabbit hutch or the length of sparkly fabric to run around the hem of your skirt. Yes, but how? Well, take any shape, flatten out its edges and measure their length. For quadrilaterals (four-sided shapes like squares and rectangles), it's pretty easy to add up all four sides. Geometry tells us that if opposite interior angles are the same, opposite sides are equal in length. For triangles, you'll need help from Pythagoras' Theorem, Sine, Cosine and Tangent... later, perhaps!

● Perimeter of a regular polygon: $2nb\sin^{\pi}/_n$
● n = number of sides; b = distance from the centre to one of the vertices
● Largest country perimeter (coastline): 202,080 km (Canada)

Perimeter

Area

■ Shape Sisters

* ✴ Provides the measure of a 2D space
* ✴ Can be applied to flat shapes and 3D surfaces
* ✴ Always measured in square units – cm², m² or km²

I love to get the measure of things, me. Just give me the chance, and I'll tell you the exact size of *any* flat shape you like, using *any* square unit you fancy. Hey, I may be square by name, but I'm not square by nature!

You already know that Line has one dimension (length). Well, I can tell you that a flat shape has two dimensions (length plus width or height). I measure the space within these dimensions – Area – by multiplying one by the other. I can tell you the size of your favourite cookie or how big a poster you need to hide that splat mark. I can also give you the area of a 3D object – Surface – by curving around a cylinder or spreading like a cloth over a laid table, accounting for every lump and bump over the plates, cutlery and candles. Oh yeah, I've got it *covered*!

* ● Area of a square or rectangle: A = base x height
* ● Area of a triangle: A = base x height ÷ 2
* ● Area of the world's largest country: 17,098,242 km² (Russia)

Area

Volume
■ Shape Sisters

☀ Measures the amount of space taken up by a 3D shape
☀ Used for measuring the capacity of containers
☀ Measured in cubic units (cm^3, m^3) or litres

There are no two ways about it, I've sure got bulk. My 3D outlines epitomize my voluptuous nature. Nobody's as good at taking up space as I am!

Let's get one thing straight: being loud is not my thing. My interest lies in how much space a 3D shape takes up, or the amount of liquid or gas it would hold if it were hollow and filled right to the brim – I'm talking capacity. I multiply a shape's three dimensions – length, height and depth – to find out. Incidentally, did you know that there are only five perfectly regular 3D shapes with equal sides, angles and matching faces? Yep – tetrahedron (4 triangles), cube (6 squares), octahedron (8 triangles), dodecahedron (12 pentagons) and icosahedron (20 triangles). Wow! My *capacity* for knowledge simply astounds me!

● Volume of a pyramid: $V = {Bh}/{3}$ (B = area of base; h = height of pyramid)
● Volume of a prism: $V = Al$ (area of cross-section x length)
● Volume and capacity: 1000 cm^3 = 1 litre; 1 cm^3 = 1 millilitre

Volume

Tessellation
Shape Sisters

* This puzzler fits shapes together edge-to-edge
* If a shape tessellates, the angles around a point make 360°
* In Latin, *tessella* means a small cubical piece of mosaic tiling

I'm a real puzzler. I just love playing around with shapes to see what patterns I can make. I fit them together so there are no gaps or overlaps between their edges.

I've been around for centuries, making intricate patterns for Islamic tile decorations, Roman mosaics and M C Escher's astounding mathematical graphic art, among other things. I can make regular patterns in a jiffy, using equilateral triangles, squares or hexagons. In a more flamboyant mood I work with two or more shapes – squares, triangles or other polygons – to make semi-regular patterns. There's a knack to making non-identical vertices add up to 360° around a given point, I can tell you! For a proper workout, I make 3D puzzles where different-shaped blocks slot together to make a solid cube. How fitting!

● Regular tessellation: shapes must fill space with no overlaps and no gaps
● Regular tessellation: shapes must all be identical regular polygons
● Regular tessellation: all vertices must look the same

Tessellation

Chapter 6
Transformation Team

Boom! Time to meet the sumo-sized movers and shakers of the maths world. The Transformation Team is a rough-and-tumble wrestling outfit, whose members excel when it comes to making a *move*. These guys are shape shifters, literally changing the way a shape looks. Each larger-than-life character has a super skill, from Translation's shove tactics and Rotation's spinning manoeuvres to Reflection's mirror images and Enlargement's resizing tricks. The Graph Gang keep all of these topsy-turvy, tumbling transformations in check. Keep in step with this lot and they'll really get you into shape!

Translation

Rotation

Reflection

Enlargement

Symmetry

Translation
Transagement Team

- ✸ Moves geometrical shapes without warping them
- ✸ Works with vector to produce sliding movements
- ✸ Size, shape or orientation of a shape remains unchanged

Ohayo! I am the Sumo Numero Uno of this outfit and my special move is the shove. I have the power to push a shape about. I don't fiddle with its size or rearrange its looks, I just slide it from one place to another. Being in the ring with me is a very *moving* experience!

My simplest transformation is to move a single point from *here* to *there*. It's a movement that has both distance and direction. Ring any bells? Yep, good old Vector helps out. Say I want to move a point with coordinates (0,3) up four and along three. Well, Vector just adds $\binom{4}{3}$ to (0,3) to get the new coordinates (4,6). Once you've mastered that little trick, you'll be pushing shapes all over the place. Just remember to give each point a shove by the same distance and in the same direction.

- ● **T**: the symbol used to denote the set of all translations
- ● Positive coordinates move a point up or to the right
- ● Negative coordinates move a point down or to the left

Translation

Rotation

Transformation Team

* Spins a shape around a fixed point – the centre of rotation
* Changes the direction in which some shapes point
* Shape remains the same size and shape

Meet Sumo #2. Konnichiwa! While Translation shoves a shape from A to B, I prefer to send it in a spin. I pick it up and twirl it around like it's a cheerleader's baton.

I don't change the size or outline of a shape, but I do alter its orientation – that is, which way up it is or whether it faces left or right. So, when I pivot a triangle, all of its corners could end up in different positions. It could look different to the way it did before rotation, although it is still exactly the same shape and size. Anything that spins – a bike wheel, say – rotates about a fixed point and that's how I operate. First I find the point about which the shape should be rotated. If the centre of rotation lies *inside* the shape it will spin like a wheel; if it lies *outside* it will act more like a bucket on a rope. Face it, I'm fab all *round*.

● Quarter turn (right angle): 90°
● Half turn (straight line): 180°
● Full turn (circle): 360°

Rotation

Reflection

Transformation Team

✵ Holds a mirror up to shapes and shows their reflections
✵ Cannot be achieved simply by sliding or turning
✵ A reflection is always the same distance from the mirror axis

I'm *flipping* crazy! I'm Sumo #3 and I'm more loony than the two heavyweights you've met so far. Konbanwa! When it comes to shapes, I'm not content just to shove or spin 'em about. No, I flip 'em right over like pancakes!

I am what happens when you look in the mirror – go on, give it a go. It looks as if your left and right sides have switched over, but this can't be the case, can it? In fact, what has happened is that the image facing you is back to front. Ouch! Instead of a mirror, I use a line on a graph – say the x-axis or the y-axis. Try to imagine that my line is the centre crease of an open book. Think of the mark a shape would leave on the opposite page if you closed the book while the ink was still wet, and you've got me! Time to pause for a little *reflection*, I think!

● Reflection symmetry: describes a shape reflected along an axis
● x=c describes a reflection on the vertical axis
● y=c describes a reflection on the horizontal axis

Reflection

Enlargement
Transformation Team

☀ Increases (or decreases) the size of a shape
☀ Action takes place around a centre of enlargement
☀ Uses scale factor to show size of enlargement (or shrinkage)

Watch out, Sumo #4 is about. Hajimemashite! Among this team's sumo superstars, I have the greatest effect on shapes – I blow them up! Pow! I slash their area. Slam!

My shape-busting moves employ a slick combination of scale factor plus centre of enlargement (COE). Scale factor determines how many times bigger (or smaller) the transformed shape is, while the COE is the point from which the enlargement is made. A line drawn through each corner of the original shape and its corresponding corner on the enlargement will converge at the COE. Uniform scaling (equal enlargement in all directions) creates an identical shape, while non-uniform scaling (using more than one scale factor) can stretch or squeeze a shape's proportions. That's me, I like to *stretch a point*!

● Scale factor of 1: no enlargement or reduction (same shape)
● Scale factor greater than 1: an increase in size (positive enlargement)
● Scale factor between –1 and 1: a decrease in size (negative enlargement)

Enlargement

Symmetry
Transformation Team

- When a shape remains unchanged by rotation or translation
- Aka reflection symmetry, line symmetry or mirror symmetry
- All regular polygons have a least one line of symmetry

Unlike the heavies of the Transformation Team, I'm more of a thinker than a doer. I study the properties of each shape I encounter, looking for a certain kinda similarity.

I draw a line down or across a shape in such a way that it has exactly similar parts facing each other. A line drawn down the centre of a square, for example, makes two identical upright rectangles side by side. Draw a line across the centre of that square and you get identical rectangles on top of one another. A line from corner to corner makes two exact same triangles, and so on. This little trick is called reflection symmetry, but I can also *turn* my hand to rotational symmetry: spin a square about its centre point and it looks exactly the same in four positions. It's perfect symmetry, I tell you, so sayonara from Sumo #5.

- Shape with the highest number of lines of symmetry: circle
- 1D shapes have a *point* of symmetry, 2D shapes an *axis* and 3D shapes a *plane*
- Opposite of symmetry/symmetrical: asymmetry/asymmetrical

Symmetry

Chapter 7
Trig-Athletes

Welcome to the ancient mathematical field they call trigonometry (from the Greek for triangle measurement). Like all things ancient Greek, the Trig-Athletes love shapes, philosophical argument and physical competition. In their world, lines come together to make Angle and three different types of Triangle. Never far away, Sine, Cosine and Tangent hang out with their old chum Pythagoras' Theorem. And what an obsessive bunch they are, as they set about finding Triangle's vital statistics – just how long are its sides? How big are those angles? And what's the area? Let's see how they're getting on...

Angle

Triangle

Pythagoras'
Theorem

Sine

Cosine

Tangent

Angle
Trig-Athletes

✷ Found at the point where two lines meet
✷ Marked by an arc and measured in degrees
✷ 360° is the angle in a complete turn – a full circle

Believe me, I'm no angel. Unless two lines are parallel, they always cross one another and you'll find me where they meet. I loiter at the corners of geometrical shapes.

I've been around for centuries: as long as 4000 years ago the Sumerians and Babylonians used to love busting their brains with me. But that's ancient history, let's get to the *point*! I come in many flavours: acute, obtuse, right, straight and reflex. When I'm acute, I'm tight, sharp and less than 90°. Obtuse sees me playing wide and loose between 90° and 180°. When I'm right (and, boy, do I like to be right), I am halfway between being acute and obtuse, at 90° exactly. And when I'm straight, I sit on Line at precisely 180°. With reflex, I blow it wide open, and flap away at angles from 180° to 360°.

● Angle of the earth's axis: about 23.5° from vertical
● Sum of exterior angles of all polygons: 360°
● Exterior angle of a regular polygon: $360 \div n$ (n = number of sides)

Angle

Triangle
Trig-Athletes

* A polygon with three vertices and three straight-line sides
* A favourite with engineers on account of its strength
* Interior (inside) angles of triangles always add up to 180°

Rigid and strong, I'm not the sort who takes kindly to being pushed around, just you *try* it. No, you'll find me reinforcing skyscrapers, bridges and dams – places that require a certain kinda supporting structure.

Geometry buffs just love me and have devoted a whole field of study with a fancy name to my spiky shapes. It's called trigonometry. My most regular form is equilateral, with all sides the same length and a 60° angle in each corner. Scalene triangles are the exact opposite with *no* equal angles or same-length sides. Isosceles triangles manage two sides the same and two equal angles, while the right-angled triangle famously has one 90°-angle corner. To work out the lengths of my sides, you need to meet my fellow Trig-Athletes. Step this way…

● Area of a triangle: $A = \frac{1}{2}ab\sin(C)$ (a, b are any two sides, C is their angle)
● Vertices of the Bermuda Triangle: Bermuda, Florida and Puerto Rico
● First triangular sandwich: 1765 (John Montagu, 4th Earl of Sandwich)

Triangle

Pythagoras' Theorem

Trig-Athletes

* The world's most proved maths formula
* Calculates the length of the sides of a right-angled triangle
* The theorem says $a^2+b^2=c^2$

I am an amazing piece of mathematical jiggery-pokery credited to one of the greatest mathe*magicians* that ever lived – the ancient Greek, Pythagoras (569–475BCE).

My mantra goes like this: "the sum of the squares of the legs of a right-angled triangle is equal to the square of the hypotenuse." Rolls off the tongue, doesn't it! OK, so let's get all things triangular sorted: the hypotenuse is the longest side of a triangle and is always opposite the 90° angle in a right-angled triangle; the legs are the two sides that make that angle. If you know the length of the legs (*a* and *b*), you can find the length of the hypotenuse (*c*), using my formula $a^2+b^2=c^2$. That's more like it!

● Number of Pythagorean proofs known to exist: 145 (*Guinness Book of Records*)
● Famous Pythagorean provers: Prince Charles; US President James A Garfield
● Famous Pythagorean triples: {a=3, b=4, c=5}; {a=5, b=12, c=13}

Pythagoras'
Theorem

Sine

Trig-Athletes

* The first of three trigonometric or circular functions
* Helps find side lengths and angles in right-angled triangles
* Remembered as SOH (Sine=Opposite/Hypotenuse)

Wave bye-bye to the shallows, my friend. Strap me and my two brothers, Cosine and Tangent, to your side and head out into mathematical deep waters.

I can show you how to get the measure of a right-angled triangle when Pythagoras' Theorem just isn't enough. Start by labelling the angles of the triangle A, B and C. The longest side, the hypotenuse (hyp), is always opposite the right angle (C). The side opposite angle A is called the opposite (opp) and the side adjacent to angle A is called the adjacent (adj). Well, I am the ratio of the opposite divided by the hypotenuse. Using the formula $\sin A = {}^{opp}/_{hyp}$, you can find out the lengths of the opposite and the hypotenuse sides when you know angle A, and find out angle A when you know the sides. It's as simple as that!

* Law of sines: $\{{}^{a}/_{\sin A}\} = \{{}^{b}/_{\sin B}\} = \{{}^{c}/_{\sin C}\}$
* Mathematical abbreviation for sine: sin
* Drawn on a graph, the sine function makes a repeating wave pattern

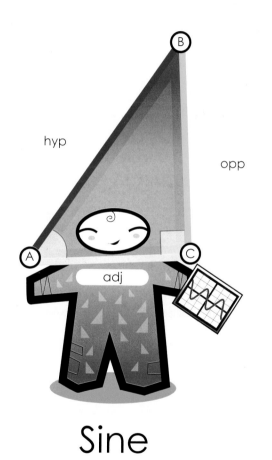

hyp

opp

adj

Sine

Cosine
Trig-Athletes

* The second of three trigonometric or circular functions
* Helps find side lengths and angles in a triangle
* Remembered as CAH (Cosine=Adjacent/Hypotenuse)

I ain't no co-star, baby. Sine might come first, but I'm never far behind. I'm known as the ratio of the adjacent side of a right-angled triangle – the side nearest angle A – divided by the hypotenuse ($^{adj}/_{hyp}$). I combine explosively with Pythagoras' Theorem to make the law of cosines, a mathematical super-weapon that holds for any triangle, not just ones with right-angles.

Cosine

● Law of cosines: $a^2+b^2-2ab\cos C=c^2$
● Mathematical abbreviation for cosine: cos
● Like sine, cosine makes a repeating wave pattern when drawn on a graph

Tangent

Trig-Athletes

- The third of three trigonometric or circular functions
- Helps find side lengths and angles in a triangle
- Remembered as TOA (Tangent=Opposite/Adjacent)

Tangent

Always direct and to the point, I'm the odd one out of the trig triplets. I am defined as the ratio of the opposite divided by the adjacent ($^{opp}/_{adj}$). But because sin A=$^{opp}/_{hyp}$ and cos A=$^{adj}/_{hyp}$, I can also be written as $^{sinA}/_{cos\,A}$. Flexible, that's me. The graph of my function doesn't drone on in endless, mind-numbing waves – it makes short flicks from negative infinity into positive infinity.

- Law of tangents: $\tan(A+B)=[\tan(A)+\tan(B)]\div[1-(\tan A)(\tan B)]$
- Mathematical abbreviation for tangent: tan
- First use of abbreviations: 1626 (Albert Girard)

Chapter 8
In the Round

Time to meet the most pleasing group of 2D and 3D shapes. Pleasing, because they are based around the perfect circle. As well as Circle himself, gallant old Circumference will give you the right royal runaround. Then there's pretty Ellipse, chunky, barrel-chested Cylinder, cocky Cone and serene Sphere! Woven into the fabric of this circular gang is the mysterious number Pi. You'll not get far without encountering this Greek letter (π) and the many mathematical formulae it finds its way into. Well, this well-rounded bunch complete our little maths adventure – we've come full circle!

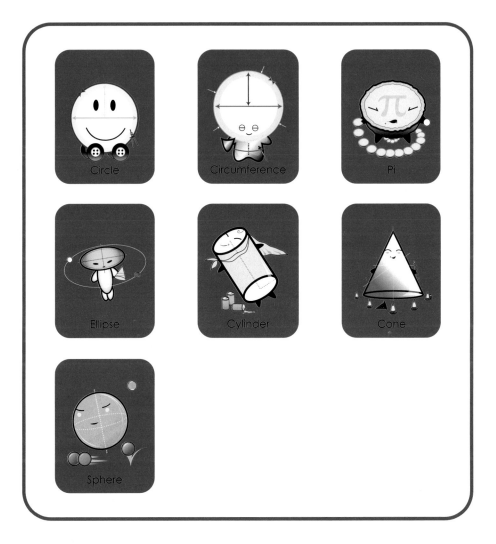

Circle

Circumference

Pi

Ellipse

Cylinder

Cone

Sphere

Circle
■ In the Round

- ☀ A perfectly round 2D shape with a talent for rotating
- ☀ Its edge stays an equal distance from its centre point
- ☀ You can draw this round, rolling Ronnie using a compass

Oh me, oh my, take a look at my ravishing rotund lines. Unique in my roundness, I simply ooze perfection. I roll along without a care in the world. Life is *wheelie* good!

My largest width runs straight through my centre and is called my diameter (*d*). My radius (*r*) is a straight line between my centre and my edge – exactly half of my diameter. I'm deeply in love with Pi, who has a special relationship with Circumference (my perimeter). But you'll meet both of them later, so let's get back to me. I am the universe's most symmetrical two-dimensional shape, with an infinite number of lines of symmetry. Just think about it – every diameter you can draw is a line of reflectional symmetry! Spin me around my centre and I look the same at all angles. Just perfect, wouldn't you agree?

- ● Diameter: $d=2r$
- ● Area: $A=\pi r^2$
- ● The Olympic symbol is made up of five interlinked circles

Circle

Circumference
■ In the Round

- ✳ The perimeter, or edge, of a circle
- ✳ When the diameter of a circle is 1, its circumference is Pi (π)
- ✳ Provides largest area of any 2D shape with same perimeter

Arise, Sir Cumference. I am a Knight of the Round and Able I am. Verily, I am the distance *around* the boundary of a perfectly circular object. Prithee roll with me as I tell thee of my gallantry and dashing adventures!

My noble status comes from my link with Circle, the most perfect of all two-dimensional shapes. The borders of all other lowly forms belong to that peasant, Perimeter. I run around wheels, toilet rolls, gas rings, megaphones and jam pots. I can tell you the length a wheel will roll in one revolution and I'm used in milometers to calculate the distance travelled by a car or on your bike. I can even tell you how much cable will wrap around a cylindrical spool (should you ever need to know such a thing). Forsooth, there's no denying I am an obliging old fellow!

- ● Circumference: $C = \pi d = 2\pi r$
- ● Arc: a portion of a circumference
- ● Chord: a straight line between two points on a circumference

Circumference

Pi

■ In the Round

- ☀ The ratio of a circle's circumference to its diameter: $C \div d$
- ☀ Denoted by the Greek letter π (say "pie")
- ☀ An irrational number that's been around for centuries

I'm a mathematical marvel, the most amazing number there is! I'm the ratio of a circle's circumference to its diameter. No matter what size circle you have, this ratio is *always* the same. I help you find a circle's area and can solve countless other maths problems.

Handle me at your peril, however, for I'm a mysterious Irrational Number. Infinitely complicated, my digits go on and on with no end. Currently, I am known to 27 trillion decimal places. As easy as π? That's as easy as 3.14159 26535 89793 23846 26433 83279 50288 41971 69399 37510 58209 74944 59230 78164 06286 20899 86280 34825 34211 70679 82148 08651 32823... *How I Wish I Could Calculate Pi* gives you the first seven decimals if you count the number of letters in each word. Chew on that!

- ● World record for memorizing pi: Lu Chao (67,890 digits)
- ● Easy approximation for pi: $22 \div 7$
- ● Better approximation for pi: $355 \div 113$

Pi

Ellipse
■ In the Round

✳ A 2D shape with a centre and two focal points
✳ Has two axes running through its centre
✳ Axes referred to as major axis (long) and minor axis (short)

A graceful oval, I bring a little glamour to the "In the Round" bunch. Imagine taking a horizontal slice through Cone – the cut end would be a circle. Now imagine taking a *slanting* slice and you get me – pretty Ellipse!

Here's a little exercise to help you understand me. Place a loop of string over two pins stuck into some thick card. Draw around these pins, keeping within the loop of string, and using your pencil to pull the loop taut as you go. Get back to where you started and there I am! The two pins mark my focal points and the combined distance from both of these to any point on my perimeter is *always* a constant. Like Circle, I have a centre. Planets use me as they swoop around the sun. I have reflection symmetry about my axes, and two-fold rotational symmetry.

● Half of each axis: semi-major axis (a) and semi-minor axis (b)
● Area of an ellipse: $A=\pi ab$
● Major axis length of the Oval Office (US President's office): 10.9 m

Ellipse

Cylinder
■ In the Round

✳ This high roller is known as a prism with a circular base
✳ A 3D favourite for containing liquids
✳ Hollow versions get used as pipes and tunnels

Captain Cylinder rolling to the rescue! I am one of the most useful 3D shapes there is. My flat bottom is great for standing me upright on level ground. This is why you'll find me used as storage: drinks cans, oil barrels, gas tanks and water butts – you name it, I bottle it.

You can figure out my surface area by opening me out – I am made up of one rectangle wrapped around two circles (top and bottom). One side of the rectangle is simply my height. The other side is equal to the circumference of the circles or $2\pi r$. My total surface area is the area of the rectangle plus the area of both circles. As well as containers and hair rollers, my hollow shape forms all kinds of wheels to move you about. Once you get the hang of me, you'll be on a roll!

● Surface area of a cylinder's side: $2\pi rh$
● Surface area of a cylinder: $A=2\pi rh+2\pi r^2$
● Volume of a cylinder: $V=\pi r^2 h$

Cylinder

Cone
■ In the Round

✳ A 3D shape that is a pyramid with a circular base
✳ Surfaces include a sector of one circle and one circle base
✳ Made by swivelling round a right-angled triangle on its base

Put your hands together, kids! Everyone loves me! Why? Because great things come wrapped in my peculiar shape – treats like chips and ice cream – or traffic cones and wizard hats!

Call me a loose cannon if you like. I am a peculiar combination of a pyramid top with a circular bottom. Cut me from apex to base and you'll find my cross-section makes two right-angled triangles standing back-to-back. If you held one of these right-angled triangles by its tip and span it round on its 90° angle, you'd trace out my strange shape. My pointed end makes me ideal at the sharp end of drills, spears and nails. You'll also find me perched at the end of your pencil after sharpening. Now that's what I call wizardry!

● Volume of a cone: $V = \{1/3\}\pi r^2 h$
● Surface area of a cone: $S = \pi r[r + \sqrt{(r^2 + h^2)}]$
● Inventor of the traffic cone: Charles P Rudebaker (1914)

Cone

Sphere
■ In the Round

* A perfectly round 3D solid that is symmetrical in all directions
* A great shape for ball games
* Half a sphere is called a hemisphere

Content and placid, I'm a bouncing ball of fun. I have no points or sharp edges – I'm one real smooth dude. My uncanny ability to roll freely in any direction makes me the best shape for playing games. I'll keep you on your toes, forcing you to chase after me or training your hand-eye coordination to connect with a bat.

Spin a flat, two-dimensional circle, say a coin, around on any diameter and you will form my beautiful 3D shape. I can be hollow inside – like a shiny bauble – but my *shape* remains solid, because it fills 3D space. Every point on my surface is an equal distance from my centre. Earth and other planets are spheres, because the force of gravity attracts equally in all directions towards a central point. Outta this world!

● Volume of a sphere: $V=\tfrac{4}{3}\pi r^3$
● Surface area of a sphere: $A=4\pi r^2$
● Number of tennis balls used at Wimbledon each year: around 50,000

Sphere

Index

Character entries are **bold**

Glossary

1D Something with a single dimension (e.g. length); a line is one dimensional.

2D Something with two dimensions (e.g. length and width); flat shapes are 2D and have area.

3D Something with three dimensions (e.g. length, width and height); solid shapes are 3D and have volume.

Arc Part of the circumference of a circle.

Axis (-es) A fixed reference line for measuring coordinates on a graph.

Constant A value in an equation that is not a variable (that is, it doesn't change: in $y=x-5$, 5 is the constant).

Cubic Any equation or mathematical relationship where the maximum value index of the variables is 3 (cube).

Decimal place The position of a number to the right of a decimal point.

Denominator The bottom part of a fraction; stands for the total number of equal parts in a fraction.

Diameter A straight line from edge to edge on a circle, drawn through the centre; twice the radius.

Divisor A number that divides into another.

Exterior angle The angle made between the outer edge of a 2D shape and the extension of the side next to it.

Focal point A fixed point, where the distances from it to any point on a curve or shape are related in a simple way (e.g. are always a constant); also called focus.

Formula A mathematical rule that is written algebraically.

Index (-ices) A small number written on the right and above a number, which tells you how many of the larger number should be multiplied together; also known as an exponent.

Infinity A number bigger than any imaginable number.

Interior angle Any of the angles inside a polygon.

Intersect When two lines (1D), planes (2D) or surfaces (3D) meet, cross or pass through each other.

Limit A value that a sum or a function approaches.

Linear An equation or any mathematical relationship where the variables are not raised by an exponent (the index is 1); a linear function always gives a straight-line graph.

Magnitude The size of a vector, found by forming a right-angled triangle with its x and y components.

Natural number The whole, positive numbers that you use to count things.

Numerator The top part of a fraction; the number of pieces being considered as part of a whole.

Parallel When lines (1D), planes (2D) or surfaces (3D) keep the same distance from each other, never touching.

Perpendicular When lines (1D), planes (2D) or surfaces (3D) intersect at right angles.

Glossary

Place value The value of a digit, depending on its position (e.g. the position of the number 2 in 20 and 200 assigns each figure with a different value).

Prime factor A factor of a composite number that is a prime number.

Prism A 3D, solid shape whose two ends are exactly the same and parallel, and whose side edges are parallel.

Quadratic Any equation or mathematical relationship where the maximum value index of the variables is 2 (square).

Radius A straight line from the centre of a circle to its edge; half the diameter.

Ratio A way of comparing two numbers; can be written as a fraction, as the first number over the second.

Real number Any number that is not imaginary.

Remainder The amount left over when one number isn't divided exactly by another.

Right angle A 90° angle.

Scale factor The value by which a shape is enlarged or reduced.

Set (as in set of all...) A group of numbers that all have something in common.

Variable An unknown number in an equation or function.

Vertex (-ices) The place where two sides of a 2D shape, or three or more faces of a 3D shape, meet; a corner.